Sink
or
Float?

What will sink?
What will float?
Make a guess.

A rubber ball floats.
Will this ball sink or float?
Make a guess. Try it out.

This ruler floats.
Will this block float?
Make a guess. Try it out.

This boat floats.
Now add some paper clips
one by one.
Will it sink or float?

A ball of clay sinks.
Now make a clay boat.
Will it sink or float? Make a guess.

This paper clip floats.
Now add some dish soap.
Make a guess. Try it out.

"Look! You can float too!"